All The Words I Never Told You

CW01081996

Emily Rumary

BookLeaf Publishing

All The Words I Never Told You © 2023
Emily Rumary

Presentation by *BookLeaf Publishing*

Web: www.bookleafpub.com

E-mail: info@bookleafpub.com

ISBN: 9789357211697

First edition 2023

ISBN 9789357211697

First Edition 2023

DEDICATION

For that person who could never voice their opinion when it mattered.

I see you, and I love you.

ACKNOWLEDGEMENT

I would like to thank my closest friends, for without them I would never have had the confidence to open my words, and heart, out to the world. Also Isaac, you have been amazing throughout this, thank you.

PREFACE

It is often when we are lying in our beds in the pitch black of night when we realise things we should've said. The words we couldn't fathom come rushing back to us with full vengeance. Often, those fleeting words hold more power, strife and feeling than we ever imagine, and more times than I can count have they not been recorded.

In writing, and poetry, I wish to give voice to the things I couldn't say in the moment. Only when we learn what we wanted to say, do we realise the significance of words. And for those speechless moments, I write to make amends with the silence.

Bonfire

Bonfire night, that special night we gather to
marvel at the infernal destruction of the things
we see no value in
Roast marshmallows over the amber flecks that
nip at our souls
We laugh, it's not that big a deal
It's all just a moment of entertainment, fleeting
away with the soot

Yet, if all I give,
Every tear of every morsel of energy,
If all of it is thrown into the fire
Crippling under the licks of blazing heat
For the masses to awe at

What is the point?
Nothing to show, but those ten minutes of
warmth
As my hard work crispens to ashes and smoke
My legacy is broken, what remains in a hollow
joke.

November 12

Chilling air outside
Shivering as you left me
When the wind grew cold

Secret.

I want that love that hugs you from behind
Trailing sweet kisses along my collarbone
The welcome home honey-smooth voice
That soothes my mind after a long day's work.

I yearn for the late nights talking
Whispering secrets,
Sweet nothings we would always keep it
Sealed off from the world, frozen in private bliss

I always wanted to stay in, you and I,
Baking in the kitchen, splashing on wine
While our friends quench their thirst in clubs all
night.
I craved to get drunk off you, find out what
made you so divine.

So why did you feed me those sweet little lies,
As if our love was a palace, something so right,
Only to break down the walls - my walls -
running in spite of it all?
You left me and our secret love, not even a
goodbye.

Stranger

I feel like I'm suffocating
In the space of the living
So much that no galaxy, not even death can
distance me enough from the burden of caring
too much.

I tied my soul, my entire being to you,
Carving out my heart so you would fit.
I skimmed down my body so my weak arms
could hold your body better, so you wouldn't
feel squashed by me,
Worked to the bone just so you could stay.
Stay for what? Me, my body, or
The fact you finally had someone who cared?

Now, stripped of everything,
I find myself wondering
Even if I could leave the galaxy
To somewhere the stars don't look like you, your
smile,
I would still be a stranger, an alien
Because once you stripped me of my old body,
You rendered me a foreigner.
Relearning, learning to be me again,
Haunted by the mirage of dead memories

That declare without you, I'm apparently just a nobody.

Maybe, just maybe,
A nobody is better than knowing you.I feel like I'm suffocating
In the space of the living
So much that no galaxy, not even death can distance me enough from the burden of caring too much.

I tied my soul, my entire being to you,
Carving out my heart so you would fit.
I skimmed down my body so my weak arms could hold your body better, so you wouldn't feel squashed by me,
Worked to the bone just so you could stay.
Stay for what? Me, my body, or
The fact you finally had someone who cared?

Now, stripped of everything,
I find myself wondering
Even if I could leave the galaxy
To somewhere the stars don't look like you, your smile,
I would still be a stranger, an alien
Because once you stripped me of my old body,
You rendered me a foreigner.
Relearning, learning to be me again,

Haunted by the mirage of dead memories
That declare without you, I'm apparently just a
nobody.

Maybe, just maybe,
Becoming a nobody is better than knowing you.

Words

I will admit
Sometimes when I crave to show people
How I feel,
My mind breaks up with my lips,
Sabotaging the relationship with not only you,
But my sense of pride.
Wordless was is only romanticised when in awe
So when I'm in agony, frustration, or simply
want more
Love melts into hate, softness boils down into a
sticky substance that spews vexation when I try
to get rid of it. It is a glue that grips my skin like
a vice, unable to stick to the things I needed to
fix

Now I'm all tied up, stewed feelings to
accompany my brewed coffee
Because I never found the words in time to tell
you what I needed to.

The artist

Beauty is fleeting
The artist forgets her name
The artwork binned.

On being present.

They say the present is a gift
That unravels as we drift through life
Yet the past sinks its talons into the previous
present, crumbling the moment into fading
memories
A trail of melancholy embedded in my history.

Closure

They say that time heals,
Scabbing the pain that once bled and gushed
through the cracks of your life
That over time it scars and eventually leaves you
fresh
To start anew
I like to pick at my scabs though,
Cursing the blood in my veins for trying to clot
Endeavouring to close up the cut that never got
clean
It will get infected, seeping into valleys of hurt
and anguish
Flooding the pain I already got struck by.
Time never healed me, it never softened my
skin, eased my heart.
Nor did it toughen me up, growing callous or
guarded.
Instead, Time seems too relative, the pain I felt
years ago sears into my soul, every time I try to
bandage my baggage Time stabs me.
Time is an ever-present ghoul, sythe in hand as it
waits for weakness
It preys on the vulnerable, those damaged by
lovers and ourselves

It prolongs our healing, gripping talons into our closure, wrenching the people we once knew. And now Time watches, silently, as I now stand, starting anew.

November

It's that time of year when the leaves flood the
ground,
Trees sparse, desolate playgrounds as the Gods
cry over the land
Washing away the summer.
November is the turning point in the year,
Turns us colder, the night overrules the sunshine
and its serene beams.
The animals scurry to hide away for Winter. The
Autumn ushers is into safety of the bitter nights.

It's also when I feel myself shedding.
That Summer haze that misted my eyes,
flurrying away as the morning fog caresses my
ankles.
November, the month where we prepare for
Christmas, in limbo of something to excite over,
It's also a time of solitude
Where I feel myself slipping into my mind
Where it's warm, guarded from the brutal
outside.
But November is isolating. Cancelling plans to
stay warm, wrapped in our minds for comfort.
Drinking hot tea like a secret elixir

That we pray will make us feel as whole as
Summer.

November, good or bad
Changes the tide for the snow and the Winter.

20.11

It's cold without you,
My bed misses your body,
Blankets fill the void.

Ghost writing

I wonder what you're doing,
Sat in bed, or out at a bar, it's beyond me
Yet I keep wondering
Like I'm the author of your book.
It makes no sense that I care too much,
Worry too much,
If you get home safe or if you found someone
else to look after.
I can't help it though, the ever-present pen in my
hand writes such intimate words, my mind's
secrets
Into letters I will never send.
A ghost writer, creating such melancholic
chapters that just never seem to end.

Forever is a moment

Forever.
The endless concept, the resin that keeps
precious things pristine.
It's the feeling of eternity
As we wish to protect those things dear to us
Keep them near to us
Never stray from us.
Yet is forever really enough?
The notion of an everlasting moment seems so
out of reach,
Forever is the thing we dream to keep
Claiming its power of preservation seems so
tactless, only daring to breach
The remarkable memories we shared.
Just enjoy the moment, savour it's feeling
For the projector in our dreams will keep
replaying
The moments that became cherished forever.

Move on, or move out.

We have to move on from those moments of
heartbreak
Let it ache, then pick yourself up
Lick your wounds while you get over it
Keep up with life as it hurls itself past,
A metro line that jolts you into action.
We don't have the privilege of stopping time,
It waits for no one. you get on board or you miss
out.
On everything.
So, as much as my soul stings from the burn of
failure
I'll step onto the train. It might take me to better
places, or not.
I'd rather be bettering myself, than realising I'm
forgotten.

Severance

My soul was bound to yours
Melded together with an invisible string
That fate played me with.
You had been my muse, my lover, my musical
summer
Every word you uttered held me hostage in a
limbo state of awe, you said you loved me for all
my flaws
Until you tricked me.
Your words burned acid into my heart, loving
whispers sizzled into cutting knives.
So I sever myself.
I untwine myself from you; I know not if you
were really once my lover or always a monster
Yet I know that wrenching myself from the
torments of your life would only end that fight,
I only ever wanted the best,
And having two hearts to take care of
Had never given me any rest.

I still have the invisible string that brought me to
you, it's golden shimmer dulled and gloom
But it'll get better, I shall use it in something
more tender,
Softer, starting new.

Flower

The daisies you so delicately picked for me
bloomed in my windowsill,
I took care of them, the sun kissed them good
morning, the water christened the petals,
The moon sang them to sleep.

I grew so attached to the small gems of the
Earth,
Looked at them just as I did to you with mirth
As they captivated my attention any time I was
near.

Now the petals weep,
Falling slowly one by one onto the ground,
It was never a plant that would keep.
Its impermanence a short spark of love in my
house.
Now I sweep the petals from the floor,
Silently eulogising how they made me happy,
How you made me happy.
They go into the bin, along with the other things
you never came back for. I weep.

The windowsill looked so barren, so dull,

I think I'll buy myself some orchids, roses, a
bouquet
And just like that, my home feels a little more
full.

Daylight

Morning.
Its decadent sunrise alluding to a fresh start,
A new day,
Full of surprise, promise of hope, love and grace
Birds chirp to your awakening, the neighbour's
cat strolling to the beat of the alarm clock
As you roll out of bed,
Out of safety,
All to work towards a better day.

At night, we scurry away from our problems,
As blind as mice, as swift as owls, pretend it is
too dark to face ourselves.
Daylight brings new prosperity,
It highlights all our flaws, all our issues,
Yet it kisses them with the soft rays of sun,
Coaxing us out of hiding
To nurture us into faith.
Daylight brings salvation
Of a clean page, cleansing us of darkness, and
embracing us in a hopeful morning of serenity.

Waiting room

Stuck in limbo, I float,
You're off with your mates, forever gloating
At the macho man portrayal you made of
yourself,
A true villain Stephen King would envy
With how you twist your knives and hide the lies
Leaving not an ounce of remorse
Fucking running off with your white horse
As your bloody hands stain the white of the
mane
And my dress

I'm sat here, painfully waiting
For the closing of a door
The ending of a chapter, or even the footnote
letting me slip out of the vice of your malicious
grip.
Nobody would believe how you shredded the
soul of an innocent teenager,
Blood washes off with enough soap.
I must tell you though, that not enough wool
could cover the eyes of all the women you
crushed,
Or keep the neighbours who heard the screams
hush, or the postman who saw the bruises.

Karma is sly, a thief in the night,
And it comes to reap what you sew,
So brace yourself for the moment your slimy
hands find themselves out of reach of the riches
you stole.
Watching in the void I shall be waiting
For the demise of your villainy
The pen that wrote your grotesque story to run
out of ink
And for people to see you for the monster you
are.
Revenge is a dish best served cold?
I'm afraid I'm too full,
But my friend Karma is never fully satiated.
They will be waiting.

Resilience

Knock one domino over, the rest tumble
Drop a flaming match, its amber fury blazes up
the room
Read one book, yearn for more
It's hard to give up and break the chain.

Fate blinds us to wrongdoings, manipulates the
Innocent into believing that we needed that.
Claims we needed that horrible pain to happen
In order to grow into 'who we were meant to
be'.

Well I call it bullshit.
Something unfathomable happens, curse it out.
Smoke the house with how you feel,
How the legacy you were building went up in
flames.
Get mad.
Don't allow for people to say it was for the best,
Only you know what is best for you…

You have to start building new blocks anyway,
don't glaze over the destruction of one thing into
another,

Don't invalidate how you felt in that moment
someone broke your vision,
Tore your heart out,
Acknowledge you had so much going for you,
have so much going for you,
Don't web over your past and make it all blue

Because your past shaded many hues
Oils, pastels, it was something designed by you.
And nobody tells you how brave it is to start
over
When the aching comfort of sleeping in the
painful remains of the what if's draws you close,
No one praises you every single day for existing
in the aftermath of the chaos,

You built your empire, and now watch it
flourish,
With nobody to thank but yourself
For picking up each domino,
Stomping out the flames on the carpet

Picking yourself back up.
It is a beautiful thing resilience;
Only our bruised souls and weary minds know
how far we went to get to finally make it
And that precious secret is worth more than any
fortune teller could predict.

Nice To Bid You Farewell

Young man on the tube with the grey long coat,
Reading a book like it had the answers to life in
its grainy paper
Listening to music I yearned to hear.
The waitress who seemed so sweet, blue eyes so
soft, yet holding such melancholy,
Indie music guy at the concert I locked eyes
with, dancing together for a fleeting few songs
before sinking into the crowd.
The flock of trendy girls in the club bathroom
telling me to get over that failure of an ex,
chanting for me to go back out to the floor and
find someone good at sex.

So many strangers, so many lives, secrecy and
intimate information veiling them from my eyes,
I only see them for an ephemeral moment, dying
to know some, ignorant of others.
Yearning straps them to my brain, post-it notes
of their character behind my eyes. Never to see
them again, yet coming back to them in the shrill
of midnight

Are they okay? I wish I had their name, kept in
contact,

Maybe we could have gone on a date?
The reluctance to speak my mind eats away at
my desperation,
Ending up a participant of a silent audience
Watching the main characters on stage get to
experience
Unimaginable things,

And all I did was watch, too shy, too voiceless to
do anything.
And now I've forgot.

Stalemate

Lucked out, kicked the curb
You pulled a bank job on me, my mind's been
jerked
Into a morbid state of oblivion
Timeless and silenced
In a void of nothingness after the words you
hurled.

I can't say I'm sorry for what I said
Or what I did,
I was pretty much dead
A zombie with a beating heart,
Nothing that could have been said
To revive me from soulless stalemate.

Somehow in the stalemate, my body stayed yet
my mind had swayed
Into a sense of solitude, sheltering its cells from
the storm of swears
Booming through my ear canals
A fury of voices beating down like thunder
Clapping in savagery

Silence and safe haven wrapped my mind up
Bubble wrapped and swaddled,

Kissing my inner child from the hatred you
swirled around like mouthwash
Cleansing your palate for round umpteen

Piece by piece,
Word by word,
My mind grew, floodgates closing
For the final time. Barriers blockading my
aching heart,
Vipers hissing at the toxins you spew.
You can't hurt me anymore.

My body was in stalemate,
But I won't play anymore,
I will not be your play date
As you cut into the fibres of my being.
I have had enough,
Pack up your chess board
It's over now, beat it.

Peace

I've made peace with myself,
Acquaintances between body and soul,
The void of desolation has been left,
Once again I'm on my own

Your mark on me has faded, a relative bruise
that purples and blues until all that remains is
The remembrance of the shackles you suffocated
me with,
Supple skin soft as before, a canvas covering the
ruined art,
Beginning again to make something better.

I left you in the void, along with the sense for
vengeance,
You're a pathetic old man,
I don't even care anymore of the resemblance
Your pitiful DNA cursed me with.
Womanhood unshackled me from the confines
of childhood naivety,
Your worst nightmare.

On occasion you try to slip out the void,
A ghost trying to haunt the house you once
infested,

You are nothing now but a fragment of a bad
dream, you become banished with the blink of
my eyes

I know that I was exiled from my past,
A veritable madwoman who emancipated herself
from the confines of honouring her elders,
Abusers.
Exultation replaces alienation, starting fresh,
Free of fear, free of pain.

I have made peace with myself for what you did
to me, who you tried to turn me into,
Peace is the water that washes over me in the
thick of night,
The soft grazing of the wind brushing through
my hair,

Peace is the female I am becoming,
Evolving into a wiser, wary woman
Thanks to the silence shut in with me
On those cold nights of alienation
I embraced the quiet, the dead of night
As the moon watches over my fragile body
A mother watching guard, scaring to dreams out
of sight.

I have cleaned my canvas of the mess you made,
Your power has waned, your time is over

I am too far out of your chokehold
For you to worm your way in.
I have peace on my side, created a new empire,
A castle of serenity, walls up too high to climb
over.

Now get off my grounds, I'm burning the
bridges
You have no right to steal what isn't yours
anymore.